D1544275

NADIA
COMANECI

NADIA COMANECI

by Gloria D. Miklowitz

tempo
books

GROSSET & DUNLAP
A FILMWAYS COMPANY
Publishers • New York

ACKNOWLEDGMENTS

The author would especially like to thank the following people for their invaluable assistance and advice: Fritz Reiter, director and head coach of Gymnastics Olympica, Van Nuys, California; Rod Hill, U.S. Olympic coach, Denver, Colorado; and Glen Sundby, editor-publisher of *International Gymnast* magazine.

PICTURE CREDITS: Wide World Photos, pages 3, 16, 23, 65, 66, 68-69, 70, 73, 77, 81, 86, 87; Rod Hill, pages 6, 9, 10, 12-13, 38, 43, 45, 58, 62; United Press International, pages 20, 22; *International Gymnast,* pages VI, 26, 74, 83

CONTENTS

CHAPTER 1

KINDERGARTEN WONDER

Nadia Comaneci (pronounced Co-man-ech) . . .

Sportswriters called her the "child heroine" of the XXI Olympiad.

A TV newscaster described her work on the bars as "swimming in an ocean of air. . . ."

Time magazine said she was as at home on the balance beam as "Br'er Rabbit in the brier patch—hopping about as if she were born there."

Nadia Comaneci—a frail-looking girl, only 14 years old. She's 4 feet 11 inches tall, and a mere 86 pounds.

But at the XXI Olympic Games in Montreal in July 1976, she became the first gymnast in the history of the modern Olympic Games to be judged perfect.

Within five days, Nadia earned the 10.0 mark seven times. She scored three 10s in the team competition, and two in the individual All Around contest. She also scored two 10s in the individual apparatus competition.

Nadia was born on November 12, 1961 in Onesti, Romania. Onesti is a city of about 40,000 people. It is near the Carpathian Mountains. Though it is an industrial city, it is lush with green trees and flowers. Nearby are rich farmlands.

Nadia's father works as an auto mechanic in Onesti. Her mother works in an office at the gymnastic training center. She has a 10-year-old brother. Her family lives in a new

Nadia smiles to the crowd as her third 10 flashes on the scoreboard.

apartment near the gymnastic school Nadia attends.

When she was 6 years old, Bela Karolyi, a gymnastic coach, came to visit her school. Karolyi had been a world champion handball player for Romania. He became interested in gymnastics when he met Marta, a gymnast, who is now his wife. Karolyi fell in love with the sport and became a coach. One of the ways he found talent was to scout the kindergartens of Romania.

The day he came to Nadia's school, he saw two 6-year-old girls playing. It was recreation period. "They were running and jumping and pretending to be gymnasts," he says. "Then the bell rang. They ran into the building and I lost them. I went into all the classes looking for them. I went again and still I couldn't find them. A third time I went and asked, 'Who likes

4

gymnastics?' In one of the classrooms, two girls sprang up. 'We! We!' they both shouted. Today, one of the girls is a very promising ballerina. The other is Nadia."

What Karolyi found in Nadia was intelligence and courage. He says, "Physically, she has strength, speed, and flexibility. Mentally, she has intelligence, phenomenal powers of concentration . . . and courage." Karolyi believes that Nadia is the best gymnast in the world. So does the rest of the world.

In modern Romania, as in the Soviet Union, sports are strongly encouraged. There are training centers for boxing, gymnastics, and wrestling. The government believes that every child should try to be good in at least one sport. The people believe that this will improve their society. Office workers, for example, stop

Nadia in class at her school in Romania.

work at 10 A.M. each day to do exercises for 15 minutes. Even the simplest books on gymnastics deal with the sport in terms of Soviet or Romanian goals.

Before Nadia became Karolyi's student, she had to pass his test. The test included a 15-meter sprint, a long jump, and a walk on the balance beam. She passed easily. "If they are afraid on the beam," Karolyi said in an interview, "we send them home right away." Nadia says she is never afraid.

Nadia was taken into the gymnastic school run by Karolyi in Onesti. There, she took regular academic classes during part of each day. After classes, she was given special gymnastic training.

Fritz Reiter, Olympic gymnastic coach from California, spoke with Bela Karolyi shortly before the

Olympics. Reiter learned that Nadia was training 3½ hours a day, giving 45 minutes to each event. But some years she was on an even tougher schedule. Up at 6 A.M., she worked out till 8 A.M. Then she went to regular school until 1 P.M. She was free from 1 until 6 P.M. Then she went back to training until about 10 P.M. If you add up the hours, you'll find Nadia couldn't have gotten more than seven or eight hours of sleep a night.

Several hundred other girls go to the school Nadia attends. Rod Hill, U.S. Olympic team manager, visited Nadia in Onesti in 1974. Hill's wife, Debbi, was an Olympic gymnast whom the Romanians admired. Hill and his wife were impressed by how tiny the young girls were.

The government says Nadia lives at home with her family. But Hill thinks

Nadia with American gymnast Kim Montagriff in English class in Romania.

Nadia takes practice sessions very seriously.

otherwise. One night Nadia and Teodora Ungureanu, her best friend and teammate, visited Hill and his wife at their hotel. It was after 10 P.M. "How did you get away from home?" Debbi Hill asked. Nadia and Teodora giggled. "We snuck out of the dorm," they said.

During this visit, the Hills speak of Nadia's great seriousness. "She is doing this for her country, we were told," Hill said. "When she was working, it was all business. No smiles. No fooling around. When Karolyi spoke, she listened. But, when she's away from the gym," Hill added, "she's just like any other little girl. Excited over chewing her first bubble gum. Curious and delighted at trying on my wife's hair curlers."

The Hills were most impressed by Nadia's perfect control and strength. "She can hit six or seven bar routines

Romanian and American gymnasts gather outside the Romanian Training Center in 1974. Can you pick Nadia out of the group?

13

in a row and not even be breathing hard."

What makes a 6-year-old willing to work so hard?

With Nadia it was a love of the sport. "At first, it was a game," she said. "But by the age of 8," her coach added, "the students must be serious about gymnastics."

Yet difficult, long hours of practice can often turn a child's love to hate. Then she needs different reasons to work so hard.

In countries such as Romania, the government rewards its best athletes for their efforts. Romania's best athletes, musicians, and artists enjoy benefits no engineer or doctor could. Though a doctor has money, he may not be able to get an apartment, or buy a car. The government makes sure the star athlete has an apartment and gives him or her a car. Most citizens, even when they can afford it, may not get permission to travel. Star athletes travel widely. They have freedoms others can't have. And so Nadia has very good reasons to work so hard. Success can mean a life she couldn't have any other way.

Shortly after Nadia began training under Karolyi, the coach selected 26 future gymnasts from his school. Nadia was one of them. With these girls he began a serious training program.

From the start, Nadia showed special abilities. She was light, quick, agile. She had the intelligence to learn difficult parts. She had the desire to work.

About a year after Nadia began training, Karolyi entered her in her first meet. In 1969, Nadia became the

Biting her nails as she waits for the judges' decision, Nadia watches the scoreboard.

youngest gymnast in the Junior National Championships of Romania. She finished thirteenth!

"Because 13 is an unlucky number," her coach said, "I bought her an Eskimo doll for good luck and told her she must never rank thirteenth again."

The next year, when she was 8, Nadia won the event. She hasn't lost a competition since.

Nadia carries the Eskimo doll with her everywhere. The doll's sealskin dress is faded now, but to Nadia it is a good luck doll. At home she has a collection of about 200 dolls. They are neatly displayed on shelves in her bedroom. "The ones I have purchased in Montreal," she says, "will remind me of my 10s in the Olympics."

CHAPTER 2

GROWING UP TO 12

Nadia came to gymnastics with several things going for her. She had good health. Her lungs and heart were strong. She had the desire to learn and was willing to work hard.

But before she could do any complicated gymnastic feats, she had to learn many basics. There would be hours of exercises to build her muscles, her endurance, and her technique.

The major part of her training included running, tumbling, simple turns and jumps, pushups, and situps. Each day, just to keep in shape, she had to do basic exercises such as somersaults again and again. Later, when Nadia finally mastered these basics, her coach began to introduce new and more complicated routines.

On the uneven parallel bars, for example, she can now do a free hip circle to handstand, followed by a Stalder. The Stalder, named after the first Swiss gymnast to do it, means she straddles down and swings up to handstand. This is very difficult to do because the body's center of gravity goes away from the bar. To master these movements on the uneven bars, Nadia practiced thousands of times. She did each part of the routine separately until it was perfect. Then she did the complete routine again and again until it became as natural as blinking an eye.

This multiple exposure photo shows Nadia's grace and agility on the uneven parallel bars.

Every competition, even on the local level, includes being judged on four abilities: performance on the balance beam, the uneven bars, the side horse vault, and on the floor.

The balance beam is 16 feet 6 inches long, only 4 inches wide, and 3 feet 11 inches high. Walking on it is a bit like walking on a tightrope. The gymnast must run, jump, turn, sit, somersault, turn sideways cartwheels, and dance on the narrow beam. It is a test of grace, dancing ability, and most of all, balance and poise. The balance beam may be the most dramatic of all gymnastic events.

The uneven parallel bars require special coordination and daring. One bar is 7 feet 6 inches high. The other is a foot and a half away from the first and 4 feet 11 inches high. Nadia had to learn to get off the bars from a handgrasp. Contestants are judged

Nadia in action on the uneven bars.

adia displaying perfect form on the balance
eam.

on how they swing from bar to bar, changing handgrasps. As a good gymnast, Nadia has to swing from the high bar, hit the lower bar with her stomach and the upper part of her thighs. Nadia seems to wrap her torso around the bar.

There are three kinds of horse vaulting—over handstands, vaults with turns, and horizontal vaults. The horse is 3 feet 7 inches high, 5 feet 4⅛ inches long, and only 1 foot wide. The gymnast must push off the horse on all vaults. She must soar as high and as far as she can. Then she must land without losing her balance.

Horse vaulting requires great strength in the shoulder muscles. Since this is a woman's weakest area, it is one of the most difficult events for women. The gymnast must have a great amount of energy through the run, then keep that energy through the vault. The vault requires hand contact with the horse. The stronger the area between a woman's shoulders in relation to her weight, the better her take-off will be. To turn around more than once while vaulting takes great courage. Nadia is very strong in relation to her weight. She also has an enormous amount of courage.

Floor exercise is a gymnastic dance routine done on a floor area 40 by 40 feet. A floor exercise should combine the skills of the acrobat and the creative expression of the dancer.

Gymnasts from the Soviet Union excel in this event. Olga Korbut, the Soviet gymnast who won two individual gold medals and a silver in 1972, was expected to be Nadia's chief competitor in the floor exercises at the Olympics.

The floor exercise may include

Like a ballet dancer, Nadia springs from the floor.

handsprings, cartwheels, pivots, and backward and forward walkovers. The athlete's feet must stay within the boundaries on the mat. Grace, originality, flexibility, coordination, and the degree of difficulty of the program count most with the judges.

Each gymnast performs for 60 to 90 seconds to music of her choice. The music is also judged. Before World War II, some gymnasts did their floor exercises to recordings of full orchestra. Now, because judges were sometimes overwhelmed by the volume of noise, the rules are different. Only one instrument may accompany the athlete.

In gymnastics, there must be a maximum of strength in the body, and a minimum of weight. Many gymnasts must work very hard to keep this balance perfect. Nadia's weight to strength ratio is perfect.

These, then, were the gymnastic exercises and equipment Nadia had to conquer. And conquer them she did. Practicing for hours each day, what before had been fun, now became hard work. Muscles hurt, then hardened and became strong. When she fell, she got up and tried again. When she hurt, or was tired, she tried not to cry. A smile from Bela or an encouraging word was enough to make her want to go on.

Fritz Reiter lunched with Nadia's coach in Tucson, Arizona about six months before the Olympics. Bela Karolyi told him that he takes the gymnasts away for one month each year. They stay at a special resort in the mountains. There, they *do no gymnastics*. Instead, they condition their bodies before their season starts.

For one month they are on a grueling, strength-building program. They run up and down hills to improve their energy, power, and stamina. They do all kinds of exercises. Then, when the month is over, they are "hungry" for gymnastics. They have some catching up to do. But along with this eagerness to get back to gymnastics, they have the added advantage of perfect conditioning.

Reiter speaks of seeing Nadia do five optional exercises without a rest, including two double-twisting somersaults, one at the start, one at the finish. He says no girl gymnast in this country can do that—five times in a row without even puffing. That kind of conditioning is very special.

Little is known about the eating habits of the Romanian girl gymnasts. Coaches who have observed the team say they eat very lightly. They seem to avoid foods with artificial additives, like salad dressing. They drink lots of milk. They eat only meat that is roasted. Candy and bread are no-nos. Once, they were seen eating chicken.

Several coaches have said that Karolyi must give the girls lots of vitamins and minerals. Curiously, they do not seem to react badly to jet lag. Most people take several days to adjust to the six to eight hour time difference between Europe and this continent. Bela's girls seem to have no such problem.

In Romania, as in all countries, an aspiring athlete begins to compete at the local level. First, she must do better than all the girls in her school. Then, better than those in her town. Then, better than those in surrounding towns. And so on, up to competitions at the national level.

After each meet, Bela would tell Nadia what she could do better. Nadia would listen very attentively. Then, she would try even harder.

She went to her first international competition three years after she began working under Bela Karolyi. She was only 9. The meet was held in Poland. She took first place in the All Around.

Soon after, she participated in the "Cup of Friendship" in Sofia, Bulgaria. There she received two gold medals for uneven bars and balance beam. When she was 11, Nadia won All Around in Romania's International Invitational Championship. In the same year, 1973, she competed with the big time—against Annelore Zinke of East Germany, and Nelli Kim of Russia. These were two of the best gymnasts from their countries.

In this "Cup of Friendship" competition, she took another All Around title.

For Nadia, the year ended on the upswing. She was awarded the first 10 in the history of the National Championship of Romania. It was no surprise to anyone that she won that championship, too.

CHAPTER 3

HARD WORK
BEFORE THE OLYMPICS

In the spring of 1975, Nadia was only 13. Bela Karolyi took her and the rest of his team to Skien, Norway for the European Championships.

Olga Korbut, the Soviet star of the 1972 Olympics, stayed home with an ankle injury. Nelli Kim had qualified for Olga's place. Elvira Saadi was the reserve.

Even with Olga out of the running, it looked like a Russian victory to the experts. Kim was a strong replacement. Ludmilla Turischeva, 9 years older than Nadia and five times a world champion, was considered the queen of the gymnastic arts. Everyone thought it would be Ludmilla's show.

But Nadia showed her boldness, courage, and abilities, even in the workouts. She went through the most unbelievable stunts. She did neckbreaking somersaults on the uneven high bar. She swung so high and far out that viewers thought she would miss the bars. Her free swing on the high bar into the handstand was flawless. "The Comaneci Come-Down" was the name given to her spectacular dismount. She releases the upper bar going face forward, and makes a half twist in mid-flight. Then, she changes direction into a back somersault before landing. For this, she was given a 9.90.

Ludmilla's confidence seemed to falter. She was first up on the uneven bars when the All Around competition began. She missed the bar with one foot in a regular sole circle. She ended up with a score of 9.35. She almost fell after a free roll on the beam and scored a low 9.25.

Nadia was as graceful and sure-footed as a cat. She did a fascinating floor exercise with two double twists, earning 9.65. On the vault, she did the best female Tsukahara ever seen by some experts. Tsukahara is named after the Japanese male gymnast who invented it. Nadia does a quarter or half turn onto the horse, then a one and a half backward somersault with straight knees. This is much harder than doing it with knees bent. For that, she got a 9.70. Her bar routine included a front somi (somersault) from the high bar, a high bar catch, two free hip circles into a half back sole circle. She let go of the bar, made a half twist, and a back somi dismount.

The crowd loved Nadia. They exclaimed with delight and amazement during her beam performance. For beam, she took a 9.75. Nelli Kim placed second; Annelore Zinke rated third. For her performance in Norway, Nadia was voted "1975 Sportswoman of the Year" by European sports writers and the IGF (International Gymnastic Federation).

Just a month before Norway, Nadia took part in the Champions All competition in London. Experts were charmed by her daring, ease, and consistency. But she didn't do quite as well as in Norway.

She began with two Tsukahara's, which seemed to "hang in the air for an age," according to *International Gymnast* magazine. Her warmup on the bars included a back somersault to regrasp the high bar and turn while hanging upside down beneath the bar in splits position. She dismounted by means of a back sole circle to half twist and back somersault.

Solemn and shy, Nadia is terribly serious about her work. Big, dark eyes dominate her pale face as she walks around between events carrying a doll. Still very much a little girl, she seems untouched by her success. Even her victory over the Soviet and British gymnasts didn't appear to touch her at all.

At the London meet, Soviet supremacy in women's gymnastics yielded to Romania's Nadia. When the scores were in, Nadia had won with a total of 37.30 (out of a possible 40) points. Ludmila Savina of Russia earned 37.10 and the British Avril Lennox took third with 36.55.

Every athlete has a stress level. If a

Nadia and a Romanian teammate watch others practice.

gymnast has a low stress level, then she or he usually quits before reaching a high standard of performance. Nadia's stress level must be very high. She performs acrobatic feats that seem dangerous and impossible. With three very important international meets coming in only a few months, the stress on Nadia must have been very great.

Two months after Norway, Nadia went to Montreal. To prove it can handle the Games, every Olympic city must stage championships in each of the events one year before the Games. Only three gymnasts from each country were invited to this pre-Olympic meet.

At the World Games in 1974, six countries had already qualified to be in the Olympic Games in Montreal. Romania was one of the six. With only 12 teams allowed, many other nations now had to compete for the six remaining spots.

Eighty gymnasts—46 women and 34 men from 17 different countries—took part in this competition. In the compulsories, Nadia and Nelli Kim were very close. Nadia led by only .20 of a point. Teodora, Nadia's friend, took third place against two Soviet gymnasts, Glebova and Koval.

In optional routines, Nadia and Kim again were almost equal. But Nadia beat everyone with her marvelous vault. Her bar and beam routines were watched with intense interest. This thin, little sprite was the giant all other gymnasts would have to better at the Olympic Games next year.

Just as in Norway, Nadia stole the show. For All Around best gymnast, it was Nadia, then Nelli Kim, and third—Teodora.

It was back to Romania after that. In the next months, Nadia rested, went to school, trained, and conditioned for the most important event in her life so far.

Then, in the early winter of 1976, Bela Karolyi entered his girls in a flurry of small meets. These would be the warmups for the big event in July.

In mid-February, Great Britain hosted the Romanians. This was to qualify their own gymnasts for the Games. Reports on the meet clearly show British wonder and dismay at the Romanian talent. "When the British girls walked into the gym on the training day and saw the Romanian first team, they felt like walking straight back out of the gym," said *International Gymnast* magazine. "The

Romanians seemed to be treating it as a mere training session. . . . After the competition, we were amazed. They didn't even march out of the gym; they just piled a few sponges under the bars and carried on working."

Karen Leighton of the British team said, "The little ones' work is so near perfection, especially Comaneci, that it all seems pointless." It did seem that way. The Romanian team placed first, second, and third—Comaneci, Ungureanu, and Grigoras.

Late in the same month, the Romanian team arrived in Tucson, Arizona for a two-day U.S. qualifying meet. Ten American girls were sent to Tucson to try for seven spots on the team. Four had been preselected. Three were to be chosen from the remaining girls. If the Americans could score within a reasonable range

Nadia at the U.S.-Romania meet in Tucson in 1976.

of the Romanians, they would have a good chance in Montreal.

As expected, Nadia accumulated the highest All Around score of 78.25. This means she averaged 9.78 on each event. Teodora followed with a 76.50 and U.S. gymnast Debbi Willcox took third place with a total of 76.15.

Fritz Reiter asked Nadia's coach at this meet where he had gained such fine knowledge of gymnastics. From books? Bela told Reiter that the best teacher "is hard work in the gym." Reiter thinks he means that the coach can learn most through observing the gymnast. Reiter spoke about Nadia and Bela's relationship. He says there is very little hugging, very little talking. They have a quiet relationship. Bela gives Nadia short, precise instructions. They seem to have a great respect for each other.

Nadia with Coach Bela Karolyi adjusting bars. They were getting ready for a test match against U.S. gymnasts in Tucson.

The day after the Tucson meet, Nadia and her teammates were in Berkeley, California. This was for the Romanian International Dual meet, a men's competition. Still, Bela's girls gave an exhibition performance that stole the show from the men.

Just before the Olympics, the Romanian team went to one more important meet. It was in May, at Madison Square Garden in New York. The American Cup 1976 gave the top men and women from 12 countries the chance to compete. On Saturday, the first day, after the optional exercises, the competition was reduced to six countries.

The next day the meet began in earnest. Fifteen thousand people showed up at the Garden. Six top men and six top women began with a score of zero. The American Cup would be awarded on the basis of that day's performance alone.

By Sunday evening, Nadia had scored another 10. She received 10 on floor exercises, 9.90 on the uneven parallel bars, 9.85 on the vault, and 9.95 on the balance beam. This gave her an All Around total of 39.70.

This meet was held on American soil. The public was pro-American. Still, the Romanian competition was hard to beat. Winners of the first American Cup were Nadia for the girls, and 17-year-old Bart Conner, an American, for the boys.

Now, for Nadia, it was on to the biggest event of her life. For eight years she had trained and worked toward this event. In July, it was on to Montreal, Canada—and the XXI Olympiad.

CHAPTER 4

MONTREAL, FIRST DAY

"The important thing in the Olympic Games is not winning, but taking part. The essential thing in life is not conquering but fighting well." Olympic Creed

It was Saturday, July 17, 1976—opening day of the XXI Olympic Games in Montreal, Canada. The city buzzed with excitement. Athletes from 94 countries would participate. Thousands of visitors from all over the world would fill the stands. Tickets, for those who had not bought early, were $100 each.

The day was balmy—warm, pleasant, slightly cloudy. The stands filled early with 76,000 spectators. And then, finally, it was 3 P.M.

With a blare of trumpets, Her Majesty, Queen Elizabeth II of England started down the red carpet. Wearing a pink dress and hat and white gloves, she took her seat in the royal box.

Then came the thrilling moment. The Greek team entered the stadium to start a parade of athletes that would last for over an hour. As each nation's athletes passed in review, musicians played their national anthem. Cheers filled the air.

Some participants dressed in native costume. The Saudi Arabians looked like sheiks. Athletes from Mali wore gold robes and white fezzes. French women marched in blue and green striped, below-the-knee dresses and capes with matching wide-brimmed hats. U.S. women wore blue pants, red shirts, white jackets, and red-white-and-blue scarves. They carried red shoulder purses.

After all the athletes had marched and the short opening speeches were finished, Queen Elizabeth rose. "I declare open the Olymic Games of 1976 celebrating the XXI Olympiad of the modern era," she said, in French and then in English.

Next, the Olympic flag was raised. The five colored rings, interlocked on a white background, represent the five continents. The colors represent the colors of flags of all nations.

The original flag, first used in Antwerp, Belgium in 1920, had been held in Munich, the site of the 1972 Olympiad. Now, the flag was turned over to the president of the Olympic Committee. He passed it on to the mayor of Montreal. Smiling, the mayor raised it high and proudly. The spectators cheered wildly.

Next came a three-gun salute. Instead of doves, 80 pigeons, symbolizing peace, were released. While the spectators held their breath, the birds cleared the roof and headed back to their owner's home, 12 miles away.

The most dramatic moment came now. A girl and a boy—Sandra Henderson, 16, and Stephane Prefontaine, 15—shared the honor of carrying the Olympic flame. Sandra, holding Stephane's left wrist, raced with him around the track. Together they lit the flame, a tradition that has been part of the Olympics for more than 2,000 years.

As the flame burned higher, a chorus sang. "Sing in praise of the Olympian Flame, lit from the rays of the sun. . . ."

A spectacular gymnastic ballet came next. A thousand young people, performing to medal-winning music, drew loud cheers. Finally, weight lifter Pierre St. Jean, 33, of Montreal took the oath for all the athletes:

"In the name of all competitors, I promise that we will take part in these Olympic Games, respecting and abiding by the rules which govern them, in the true spirit of sportsmanship, for the glory of sport and the honor of our teams."

The Queen left. The athletes marched out. The Games could begin.

The Olympic Games date back more than 2,000 years. In 776 B.C., 45,000 Greeks crowded the stadium at Olympia to watch and cheer. The first victor on record won the 200-

yard race. He was Coroebus, a cook from a nearby city.

From that year on, the Olympic Games were held every four years for nearly 1,200 years without a break. Not even wars could interfere with the Games. On the day of the Games in 48 B.C., for example, Greeks were battling invading Persians. Still, at Olympia, the stadium was alive with sports fans watching the finals of the boxing tournament.

The development of physical strength and skill was the real purpose of the contests. No heroes received greater praise—not even generals who were victors in great wars. Each victorious athlete was crowned with a wreath of wild olive. His name was honored throughout the country. Whole cities turned out to welcome him home.

Only free-born Greek citizens could compete. From these, only the best athletes, who had passed many trial meets, were selected to go to Olympia. There, for 10 months, they trained under professional coaches and trainers. They lived in the gymnasium and practiced all day, every day. There was no time off for relaxation or pleasure. At the end of that period, they were ready for the Games.

When Greece declined as a world power, the Romans took over the Games. But under the Romans, the amateur spirit and religious atmosphere changed. The big cities began hiring professional athletes, instead of amateurs, to compete. The lowest point came when Nero, the Roman emperor, entered the Games in 67 A.D. In the 10-horse chariot race, he fell. The officials helped him up and put him back in his chariot. Then they gave him first prize.

The Games were stopped in 394 A.D. Theodosius I, Christian emperor of Rome, said they were a pagan festival. Soon after, barbarian invaders robbed and destroyed the Olympic buildings. Finally, earthquakes destroyed what was left.

The modern Olympic Games began on the afternoon of April 6, 1896. A crowd of 50,000 sat eagerly in the rebuilt Stadium of Herodis in Athens. Many thousands more sat on the grassy slopes of nearby hills.

Ten Americans went as the American track and field team. Only one of the 10 was a national champion (Tom Burke, a quarter-miler from Boston). The Americans competed against 12 nations in Athens. There were 12 track and field events on the program. The Americans entered every event except the 800-meter run. They scored nine victories in 11 tries.

But not until 1912 did the modern version of the Games, the way we know them, really take hold. Then, in Stockholm, the Swedes set the example for all Games to come.

For centuries, women were not allowed to see or take part in the Games. Those who disobeyed were hurled off a cliff. Pherenice, a noblewoman and widow, was the first female to see the Games and live to tell about them. She had taken over training her son, a runner, when his father died. When the son was accepted to compete in the Games, Pherenice disguised herself as a man. She slipped into the stadium and saw her son win his race. She became so excited that she screamed with joy, rushed onto the field, and kissed the boy. Her voice and actions gave her away. She was arrested, tried, and found guilty. But her life was spared because of her plea of motherly love.

Eventually, women were allowed to see the Games. Under the rule of the Romans, women were even allowed to compete, but only in chariot races.

The first women to participate in the modern Olympic Games were six females who took part in the game of lawn tennis. This was in 1900. Archery and figure skating for women were part of the London Olympics in 1908. Swimming was added in 1912 and fencing in 1924. In 1928 in Amsterdam, women competed in gymnastics and track and field for the first time.

Today, women compete in many Olympic sports. Gymnastics is dominated by women. Their scores are usually better than those of the men.

In the year before the Olympics,

Preparing to go on the bars at Montreal in 1976,
Nadia is deep in thought.

Nadia had been to many international meets. Still, the excitement and pageantry of the Games was something very special. Her performance there would matter a great deal—to her family, her coach, her team, her country. And most of all—to Nadia.

CHAPTER 5

10.0!

An Olympic gymnastic meet is like a four-ring circus. The beam and the bars rise up at either end of the field. In between, side by side, are the vault and the floor exercise area.

Usually, all four areas are in use at once. One gymnast may be doing somersaults on the beam. Another may be doing an Evel Knievel-type twist on the vault. Another may be swinging like a monkey around the uneven bars. And a fourth may be doing an acrobatic ballet to piano music.

As each girl comes off the apparatus or floor, her coach usually embraces her. When the gymnasts rotate to their next station, a recorded march is played. Off the girls go in single file—tiny, slender, graceful performers.

Nadia and her teammates were skilled. But they knew the real competition would come from the Russians. There was Ludmilla Turischeva to deal with. She was the true champion in Munich four years before. There she took the medal for combined exercises, the most honored of the individual events.

There was Olga Korbut, darling of the 1972 Olympics. Besides the two individual golds and a silver, she had shared a gold medal as part of the Russian team. She had done more to spread interest in gymnastics than anybody in recent history.

Nadia's coach gives her last-minute instructions at Montreal.

There were Nelli Kim and Maria Filatova, Carola Dombeck of East Germany, and Marta Egervari of Hungary. And there was Nadia's oldest friend, the pixie-like, bubbling Teodora Ungureanu, 15.

On the first day of competition, Sunday, July 18, women gymnasts were judged as a team on compulsory exercises. Points were awarded on how well each performed *prescribed* movements on beam, bars, horse vault, and floor.

In the optional exercises the next day, judging would be based on how difficult and original a program Nadia and her team could perform. The compulsory part of the program tests how competent a gymnast is technically. The optional exercises show off her special talents.

Ten—the top score possible—had never been achieved. In fact, the

scoreboard was not even program-
med to show a 10. There would be
four judges. The high and low scores
would be thrown out. To get a 10.0,
the middle scores both had to be 10.0.

Nadia became the first woman in
the history of Olympic gymnastics to
make a perfect score.

On that first Sunday, she did it on
the uneven parallel bars. It was the
first of four 10s she would make on
the bars within the week. At times,
Nadia's body seemed to freeze above
the bars. Then she would rocket
around and under the bars in a blur
of arms and legs. She was a bird in
flight, soaring, dipping, hovering,
flying. Where others hesitated, Nadia
became bolder. The crowd knew they
were seeing an extraordinary per-
former. They gasped and cheered.

Nadia dismounted. Her face broke
into what many considered a mechan-

Nadia swings perfectly between the uneven parallel bars at Montreal.

ical smile. It was not the grin of delight that Olga Korbut could show—a smile that won affection. "I know how to smile, but I'm here to work," Nadia said later when asked about this.

By Monday night, she had received two more perfect scores. One was on the balance beam, another on the parallel bars.

Many feel she is best on the balance beam. Ninety seconds is a very short time. In that brief time Nadia performs many movements with great skill and speed. This is what she does: a jump to straddle, one leg up in an L; presses to a handstand, then a one-fourth pirouette and step down; skips and steps, kicks again to a back flip-flop step out; more steps and full turn backward; a body wave, dance steps, pose and aerial forward; side aerial to flip-flop step out, leap; lies down on

Waving to the crowd, Nadia is truly happy with her Olympic gold medal.

This multiple exposure study shows Nadia's graceful movements on the balance beam at Montreal.

The sign flashes a 10 at Montreal and Nadia jumps with joy. It was her third perfect score of the Games.

beam, does a Valdez through a back walkover to a knee perch, cartwheels to a stand; a back walkover to a handstand in the split position; two flip-flops; split leap, body waves; a round-off, double twisting somersault dismount!

Nadia is able to show great concentration. On the Forum floor Monday night, four events were going on at once. While Nadia was performing on the beam, a pianist was playing for a floor exercise 30 feet away. The crowd was cheering as someone performed well on the parallel bars. Nadia says she does not hear these noises. "I think so much of what I must do," she said.

At least three times Monday night, Nadia and Olga Korbut were performing at the same time. Experts said Olga was as good as she had been in Munich. But a foot injury slowed her a bit. And more important, the crowd was rooting for Nadia.

After her performance, Nadia said, "I was very glad, but I've done it (gotten 10s) 19 times (in other meets). And my teammates are always helping me."

The proud Romanian officials held a press conference later. The press room at the Forum was noisy and crowded. Reporters shot questions at tiny, shy Nadia.

"Would you like to travel around the world on an exhibition tour?" she was asked.

"I want to go home," she said through an interpreter.

"Aren't gymnastics fun?"

"It is work," she said. "They once were fun—like playing a game. But now I must work very hard."

Nadia said that though she had

Nadia won the gold medal and Russia's Olga Kor-but the silver in the balance beam event.

Strain shows on Nadia's face as she completes a perfect routine.

made two perfect scores, she would try to do better. "Hard work, perseverance, courage and grace" make a good gymnast, she said.

When asked who her strongest competitor was, she surprised reporters. Was it Nelli Kim, Ludmilla Turischeva, or Olga Korbut? No. She said her strongest competitor was her friend and teammate, Teodora Ungureanu.

Saying goodbye to reporters, she spoke in French. "Je remercie beaucoup la publique Canadienne." (Again I thank the Canadian people very much.)

The next morning, Nadia walked around the Olympic Village with her teammates and a couple of chaperones. She signed autographs and posed for a few pictures.

Another press conference was held on Tuesday. Nadia entered the room with her coach and Teodora. She wore a lavender pantsuit and her hair was tied in a pony tail. Reporters and photographers surrounded them.

Nadia seemed embarrassed by the attention. "I came here to do gymnastics, not to be interviewed," she said. She sat straight in her chair during the questions. She rarely smiled.

When asked who her idol was, she and Teodora giggled. It was Alain Delon, the French actor, she admitted.

One reporter said she might be copying Olga Korbut's showmanship on the bars and beam. "Showmanship is not the best term," Bela Karolyi said. "Her style is the Romanian style. We are not copying anybody."

Reporters and those who have met Nadia say that she likes school and is a good student. She finished eighth grade this year with an 87.5 average.

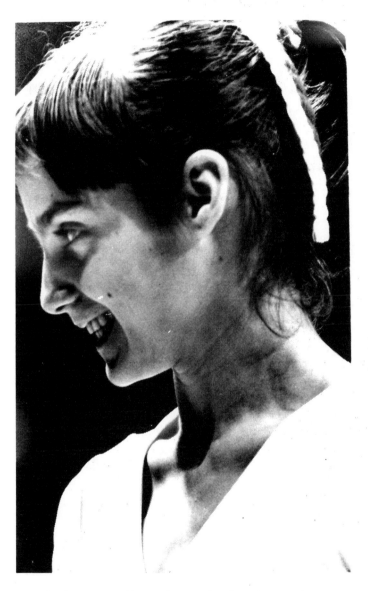

Nadia is all smiles after winning her third gold medal at Montreal.

Besides the usual subjects, she studies Russian, French, and English. Her favorite English words are "hamburger" and "okay." She enjoys swimming, skiing, and collecting napkins and placemats from different countries. She also enjoys her doll collection. At the Games she often hugged her Eskimo doll.

It must have been very hard for Nadia to fall asleep Monday night, after the excitement of the past two days. But Tuesday was an easy day, devoted to men gymnasts.

What would she have thought about in those restless minutes before sleep on Monday? She was probably looking ahead to Wednesday. Wednesday would be a very important day. She would be one of her country's three top performers. On Wednesday, the All Around Finals for Women would be held.

CHAPTER 6

AND MORE 10.0s!

Until Wednesday, Nadia was competing as part of her team. Her score was counted in with the scores of her teammates. Now, it was each gymnast for herself. The best three Romanian gymnasts would compete individually against the top three gymnasts of each of 11 other countries. The individual who got the highest score would take the All Around Best Gymnast medal.

Sports writers had thought it would be a battle between Nadia and Olga Korbut. But the real competition was between Nadia and Nelli Kim of the Soviet Union.

Nelli Kim took a perfect 10 on the vault. She pushed off to an unbelievable height. When the score was posted, she didn't even seem to realize what she had done. But, as the crowd cheered louder, she looked up, grinned, and waved. Turischeva and Dombeck of East Germany took second and third for the vault.

Nadia electrified the 18,000 spectators on the uneven parallel bars. Olga, warming up for the balance beam, stopped to watch. She showed no reaction as Nadia took her fourth of the seven 10s. The crowd cheered wildly.

When Nadia was on the beam later, Olga was nearby, but did not watch. Another 10, the third for balance beam. The crowd began screaming again. While the spectators roared

A perfect flip from the balance beam wins Nad another Olympic gold medal.

their delight, Olga had to start her floor exercise.

On an earlier day, in floor exercises, the East Germans had done their routines to "Deep in the Heart of Texas." The Hungarians danced and tumbled to "When the Saints Come Marchin' In."

Wednesday, Nadia did her floor routine to "Yes, Sir, That's My Baby." It was saucy, fun—but it didn't have everything Nadia could give. For floor, she earned 9.90, behind Kim and Turischeva.

When Nadia was declared All Around winner, she went up to the winner's platform. She climbed to the highest position while the band played the Romanian national anthem. Beside her, taking the silver medal, was Nelli Kim. Ludmilla Turischeva, who had taken All Around in 1972, kissed Nadia lightly.

Nadia completing her floor exercise with a perfectly timed strut and smile.

Turischeva climbed to the third position for the bronze medal.

There was one more day to go. In Thursday's meet, only the top two performers of each country were eligible. Only six athletes were allowed for each apparatus or event. This was the Individual event finals.

There was no stopping Nadia. Though she didn't do the most difficult routines she knew, she still earned 10s. She took two more gold medals, one for the uneven bars and one for the balance beam. Both were 10 performances. She also took a bronze medal for floor exercises.

The night belonged to Nadia and Nelli Kim, 19. Kim won the floor exercise with a perfect 10 and took the vault, her specialty, with a 9.95. Olga Korbut won only one individual medal—silver for the balance beam.

Nadia's performance on the uneven bars was the highlight of the evening. She whipped her body from bar to bar like a fairy flitting from leaf to leaf. People held their breath waiting for her thrilling back somersault, the "Comaneci" dismount.

With Thursday's performance, the women's gymnastic events came to a close. The score was in.

All Around—1. Comaneci. 2. Kim. 3. Turischeva.

Individual Floor Exercise—1. Kim. 2. Turischeva. 3. Comaneci.

Individual Vault—1. Kim. 2. Turischeva. 3. Dombeck.

Individual Uneven Parallel Bars—1. Comaneci. 2. Ungureanu. 3. Egervari.

Individual Balance Beam—1. Comaneci. 2. Korbut. 3. Ungureanu.

Team—1. U.S.S.R. 2. Romania 3. East Germany.

What now for Nadia? What does a

The Soviet Union's Ludmilla Turischeva kisses Nadia for winning the gold medal for overall performance in gynmastics. Ludmilla won the bronze.

Homeward bound, Nadia carries a few souvenirs onto the plane at Montreal.

14-year-old do for encores after an Olympic medal sweep?

For now, Nadia was going home. She would vacation at a Black Sea resort. Of the future, she said, "I want to learn new things."

Nadia will probably be back for the 1980 Olympics. She will be 18 then, still young enough to keep her crown as best woman gymnast in the world.

But after that? Olympic athletes from Soviet countries often become coaches in their sports. That way, they can develop talent even beyond their own for their countries. Nadia is a very bright girl. Whether she will go into coaching, or turn to some other interest, no one knows. Not even she. Only time will tell.

GLOSSARY

Balance beam—this is 16 ft. 6 in. long, 4 in. wide, and 3 ft. 11 in. high; gymnasts run, jump, turn, sit, somersault, turn sideways cartwheels, and dance on the beam.

Compulsory exercises—these are used to show a gymnast's technical competence, with points awarded on how well prescribed movements on the beam, bars, horse vault, and floor are performed.

Exhibition performance—when a team of gymnasts performs for entertainment, rather than in competition.

Floor exercise—a gymnastic dance routine performed on a floor area 40 x 40 ft.

Horse vault—this is 3 ft. 7 in. high, 5 ft. 4½ in. long, 1 ft. wide; there are three basic kinds of horse vaulting: over handstands, vaults with turns, and horizontal vaults.

Individual All Around contest—gymnasts are judged on their individual performances on all of the apparatus, rather than as part of a team.

Individual apparatus contest—gymnasts are judged on their performance on the beam, bars, horse vault, and floor individually.

Optional exercises—the gymnast chooses and performs a series of exercises to show off his or her special talents.

Stalder—a move used on the uneven parallel bars in which the gymnast straddles down and swings up to handstand; named after the Swiss gymnast who was the first to do it.

Tsukahara—a move used in horse vaulting, named after the Japanese gymnast who was the first to do it; the gymnast does a quarter or half turn onto the horse and a one and a half backward somersault with knees straight.

Uneven parallel bars—two bars placed one and a half feet apart, with one bar 7 ft. 6 in. high and the other 4 ft. 11 in. high; gymnasts are judged on how they swing from bar to bar, changing handgrasps.

Valdez—a move used on the balance beam.